A LITURGY FOR STONES

Lora —
Hope you enjoy
these liturgies.

Peace
[signature]
11 May 2003

A LITURGY FOR STONES

DAVID WRIGHT

DreamSeeker Books
TELFORD, PENNSYLVANIA

an imprint of
Cascadia Publishing House

Copublished with
Herald Press
Scottdale, Pennsylvania

Cascadia Publishing House orders, information, reprint permissions:
contact@CascadiaPublishingHouse.com
1-215-723-9125
126 Klingerman Road, Telford PA 18969
www.CascadiaPublishingHouse.com

A Liturgy for Stones
DreamsSeeker Books is an imprint of Cascadia Publishing House
Copublished with Herald Press, Scottdale, PA
Library of Congress Catalog Number: 2002192810
ISBN: 1-931038-13-9
Printed in Canada by Pandora Press
Book design by Cascadia Publishing House
Cover design by Gwen M. Stamm
Special thanks are offered to Jim Schietinger for permission
to use his photograph on the cover.

The paper used in this publication is recycled and meets the
minimum requirements of American National Standard for Information
Sciences—Permanence of Paper for Printed Library Materials, ANSI Z39.48-1984.1984

Grateful acknowledgement is made to the editors of the following publications
where many of these poems appeared or are forthcoming:

*Avatar Review, The Christian Century, Dream Seeker Magazine, Gangway, Mars Hill
Review, Mennonite Life, The Mennonite, Prairie Poetry , Rhubarb, re:generation quarterly,
Savoy Magazine, Teaching English in the Two-Year College, 3rd Muse, 2 River View,* and
Red River Review. "Chicken Scratches on the Back of Sunday's Bulletin"
also appeared in *Lines from the Provinces* (2000).

The author thanks the many readers who have offered substantial feedback on these
poems, especially those at Richland Community College, Wheaton College, and *The
Avatar Review.* An additional note of gratitude is due to LaSalle Street Church, First
Mennonite Church, and Lombard Mennonite, faithful communities who made space for
a poet to worship and work.

Library of Congress Cataloguing-in-Publication Data
Wright, David, 1966-
    A liturgy for stones / David Wright.
      p. cm.
    ISBN 1-031038-13-9 (alk. paper)
    I. Title.

PS 3623.R534L5 2003
811'6--dc21

                                        002192810
10 09 08 07 06 05 04 03   10 9 8 7 6 5 4 3 2 1

The impassive stones that receive and return so many echoes,

The souls moving along. . . . are they invisible while the least atom of the stones is visible?
—Walt Whitman

Contents

Afterword

A LITURGY FOR STONES

Altar Piece

The extraordinary patience of things! —Robinson Jeffers

The rhythm could not be simpler:
clicking of rock on rock.
the mason's hands marry stones
to the particular stones he finds,

clicking of rock on rock
building and built by habit.
To the particular stones he finds,
he gives a blessing of mortar,

building and built by habit.
He lays odd pieces aside before
he gives a blessing of mortar.
Surfaces turn, find their places in time.

He lays odd pieces aside. Before
the mason's hands marry stones
surfaces turn, find their places. In time,
the rhythm could not be simpler.

1

Like Trees Planted by Streams of Water

On this small bluff, lives hang like leaves.
A psalm trickles and surges
in roiling eddies and worried curves.

The Illinois could erode the banks.
All the new and old oaks could tumble
into a templed dam. But roots twist hard

instead beneath the river's silted bed.
They fill and feed the farthest leaves
that burn until lives fall to the water

in flames. The colors catch and wither
in human debris. Between a milk carton
and one rented ski, a single, silver fish

breaks the gray-green surface of its world,
like a tiny god might puncture the sky.

Children's Sermon

The children are angry.

The story is too sweet,
too much about love, Jesus,

being kind to neighbors. No
prophet's head offered

on a king's platter like a giant
frightened apple. No one suffers

God's wrath. No cities burn
to fine ash as sulfur slides

down heaven's holy sluice
to drown the wicked. No one

grapples God to a draw. A woman,
(voice smooth as her pressed

flower-print skirt) displays pictures,
all the colors of children possible,

arranged on Jesus' lap like strange
construction paper bouquets, faces

like cotton blooms tucked over
her prim legs. Adults laugh at restless

bodies, cringe as a stocky blonde boy
wanders behind the woman, so even-
toned and unaware, as he performs
practiced karate chops and forms

high kicks over her head. His mother
eyes him from the third pew; he grins,

kicks, grins, kicks, until she clears
the steps in a terrible blur to collect him.

She contains his flailing limbs in a sweep
of her long mother's arms. He tries

to cry, but she smothers his voice
in her own flowered breast.

The children sit still.

They have glimpsed God's mighty arms
filled with their brother, have seen God's

long reach. They believe God's hands
could gather them up for good.

Swallow Song

A drop,
a drop
of the praise
in the plate,
and a clink, clink,
clink of the plate
on the altar, clink
altar, two
plates full
of drops, drops of praise
raised and dropped
in the plate.

For a drop
I squeeze.

Drink, gulp, drink
dribble,
I swallow
lies, pride, lies
for a drink.

Church Janitor

After the baptism I cleaned out the tank,
walls still slick with redemption.

The drain guzzled its holy deluge;
bristles of a broom vibrated

the fiberglass floor. I raided the closets
for solvents, but nothing, even scrubbing

on my knees, could erase dark prints
from the pastor's black shoes, real marks,

not mythical but material, permanent
from wherever he stepped before church

showing exactly where he stood as, one by one,
he dipped bodies backwards into heaven.

At the Mennonite Talent Show

Two men in drag sing "Stand By Your Man."
They shaved and changed during dinner
so they would not be recognized, and
here they stand, by each other, thinner

without mustaches and beards. Flashes
light the room so that two, three years
from now we can laugh. A tray crashes
in the kitchen, so loud, no one can hear

the sweet harmony these now lovely men
make on the chorus. We are all sober.
We are not allowed to be drunk when
we have this kind of fun. We must over

come all our inhibitions by sheer will
and surprise. The skits, the songs
must be so much better for us to still
a room full of conscience, the wrongs

of our lives, our world, so much in mind.
Some eyes and shoulders cannot untense,
even with permission. How to unwind
our taut, wound hearts? How to commence

celebrating talents when the humble
should be exalted, when the proud
will be brought low, made to stumble
along like men in heels before a crowd?

Electric Glossolalia
(The Neighborhood Boys Speak in Tongues)

We would sometimes hold
a red battery, nine volts,
against our tongues,

pressing for interminable moments,
until power's metal flavor,
its stunning signature wrote

itself into our neurons,
flared across synapses.
But Sam always recused

himself, always went to fix
something to eat, maybe a slice
of cheese between parallel

slabs of white bread.
We dared each other to endure
longer. We worked hard

on the nuanced expression
that can mask a ten-year old's
crazed kaleidoscope of pain

and glee. And Sam stood,
chewing his sandwich
savoring American cheese

and Wonder Bread
while his friends tasted
electricity and explained

to him how it felt to dare.
Still he stayed mute and stared,
refusing to translate

our numb tongued languages of joy.

For John

mounds timbers points
groves islands savannas
a language of prairies
 —John Knoepfle, "east in mclean county"

We talked over words,
inside them, about twisted
roots, articulate land,

but I could have better
listened—again—
to the lilted languages

and tindered skies
caught tight and taut
in your memory's

frugal, generous eye.
Look—again—my foot
keeps time under my

chair, taking steps
in place, in place
in places I go through

when—instead—like you
I should dance the dirt
down deep with measured

steps, and stay.

My Friend at Firestone Asks about Poems

You got any with forklifts in the middle?
Maybe some lines about solvents applied
to assembled tire beads or rubber coated steel wire?
Or about treadstock, or how lunch tastes
at midnight when your nose and throat
burn black, your hands feel like green tires,
waiting to be molded and cured? Anyone write
how good a football game looks on Sunday
at eleven-thirty when you've come off twelve-hours,
slept for three, maybe four, and settled
into a recliner, settled into three or four High-Lifes
to watch a batch of ham fisted boys
batter themselves against a sodded field,
against other huge sons of bitches who should be
throwing tires themselves if they weren't big
as Buicks? Got any stuff with layoffs
and new fishing boats on credit that, dammit,
no one will take back because they can't be sold
anyway? Your poems got room for a forklift,
a football game, unbreakable cement, new solvents,
lunch at midnight, a place to recline?

Looking at Roadside Bluestem Before Leaving Decatur

1.
A littered gully fills with tire carcasses, beer bottles, a bed of
    random gravel, and two nailed pieces of green
    painted two by four.

The air tastes thick, too heavy with factory drafts—
    burnt rubber, roasted soybeans, yeast, and corn
    distilled to nectar.

God we love what they send on the wind,
    what we leave in the gullies,
    what they leave in our pockets,
    what they leave in our lungs.

We love this scent of money, the dry, paper taste on the backs
    of our tongues.

We love these old plants while they live.

2.
Against blue-purple culms, silk filaments catch backlight.

Against blue but septic skies, forage grass appears
    from attention and neglect.

The copper colored turkey claw gives the universe the finger.

Fires in the Fall smooth the dry horizon but will not flare
    to where these seeds, their tender shoots lurk,
    buried under prairie,
    buried under gullies running over,
    buried after frost to rise in April.

We want to love the native grass, taller than a woman,
    tall as any man.

We want to stay where bluestem roots, gnarled as human nerves,
    prosper under blackest dirt,
    refuse to wither during winter,
    drink from sources purer than the air.

Spring Burn

Nothing appears complete,
the stalks and stubble
of last fall's crops, unmended
fences of the empty pasture.
Railroad ties burn along the tracks—
a pile of tarred and flaming wood.
A farmer left his pitch fork
in the ground then walked away.
Top soil dissolves in the wind,
obscures the small sky.
Like a beloved's last morning
fixed in memory, each gesture
too exaggerated, these flames
flare against the cold April air
and could be sails, could catch
the wind and slide down
the smooth iron rails to a city.
Not joy, or grieving, the past
arrives as light and invincible
as skin. It begins in our eyes,
or the ground, and gives way
to a flame becoming itself, or the sun.

2

♣

Gammal Fäbodpsalm

The deep backward bending of the prairie grass
makes this nineteenth century woman
think of sailing, of how sick the ocean
made her, her daughter, how she would ask

her husband for fresh water, how he'd descend
to a dark hold below their own and return
too long later, her throat so burned
by then she could not speak. At the end

of the gray blanket of sky, came riding
across Ohio with blank German women, a pair
of young Norwegian men who held their
arms tight to their sides as if hiding

parcels. Then, this Illinois sea, a lightning
covered sky, and twelve foot high stalks
knit so tight at the root it took an ax
to bring them down. Down in the tightened,

dense weave of the bluestem, she felt
her way to a clearing. Down in the thick
dirt she dug her way to a root ball, sick
again with a dream that she had left

her daughter on that ship. Staring down
from a moraine, she sang in Swedish,
Gammal Fäbodpsalm; she said in English,
Now. And waded into the limitless, unmown

acres of terror and comfort, the hymn
and the vision of a Småland pasture
full in her forehead with those four

months, the child's blanket, unpinned

like a sail as she fell through the calm,
like a sail as leaden as an old, bleak psalm.

In the Language of Dreams

Early mornings I navigate sleep's shore,
almost land, until a delinquent dream
appears like a watery hand and draws me more
and more back to deep, deep heavenly streams
where a waif of a child watches me and sings
from a tree, a golden birch that grows high
in the middle of a river. He swings
thin white arms through the wounded morning sky,
keeps perfect four-four time to my breath, breath,
breath, breath. His voice, richer than his years,
echoes against my inner ear. "O Death,"
he sings, "O Death." Of course he shows no fear
as currents rise to his branch, reach his chest.
A world waits, and wakes, just as waters crest.

Still Life: Orbs of Delight

Hover, not exactly round, but alive
in the air of paint, always ready to fall
on the bed clothes. The texture, perhaps,
what Eve saw, what Adam felt but lost
when, bored, they reached to take such
orbs into rough and actual hands.

Elegy (for David Erlanson)

You seemed to always know what you were doing, David,
leaning in your office chair, always leaning back at peace,
attached to a place beyond us, where you could not be reached
by the petty bickering of committees or your own unease.

I hear, though, they dug up empty Smirnoff bottles,
forgotten in the crannies of your basement like lost tools,
for years after a friend rescued you from them. The labels,
readable,were scratched at the corners where you peeled

them as you drank away some certainty or other,
perhaps an emptiness like your office shelves,
so bare of books we all have pilfered, after
catching ourselves scanning titles for the self

who would have loaned them at a loss. I cannot eulogize again.
No one better ask, not after you, my father, my grandfather.
I have no more smooth words to bury men I recognize,
only my own cellar piled with books, bottles, hammers

I cannot return. No, I would rather rattle rougher words
to scare and scatter all these deaths, like starlings from the curb.

Tending Gardens

1.
He died and left a lovely world of sculpted,
bricked off beds in the backyard, leaky sprinkler
pipes snaking from the house to the boundary

bushes. Peonies, herbs, purple coneflower,
columbine, and mint, mint everywhere.
In the fall I trimmed lilacs by the drive,

pruned them back to bare, gray branch,
as my mother watched. She didn't know.
I'd never learned. He never said: don't trim

them late or come the spring no purple thing
will scent the wet world. Next year, though,
we wait, without an oracle. They blossom.

2.
Weekends my wife waters. She weeds.
She comes into the house filthy and free
of burdens. She laughs and sighs and arranges

her tools and says nothing. I suspect her
ornamental grasses hide knowledge,
something wild as pleasure.

When I rake through them in the morning,
I find no small, red fruit in the soil.
Nothing there to elude my unskilled hands.

I could dig here all day, jealousy dripping
from me like sweat. I could. But fall will come
and silver these tall grasses. We'll see then what lives.

Blind Willie's Wife

Broke bottlenecks for him, told him, tune to open D,
told him, Willie quit growling that gruff, fake bass,
let your sweet tenor take off and ride.

She would harmonize, then break him another
bottleneck, grind it down quick on a cement stair,
leave little glints of glass dust on his shoes.

She knew his hands, way he thumbed the bass line,
knew his voice and how he couldn't keep from crying,
how, together, they'd give over to gospel and slide

right up the string, Lord, right up the string,
smooth as Willie's finger in a bit of broken glass.

After Bach's Air in G, Transcribed for Flute

Everybody rides the air,
the starting and stopping,
the fluttered tongue of a trill
would be nothing without breath
beneath the muscle. To push
a phrase into the plain church
takes faith in sound, in the body,
takes lips pursed, unpursed above
the silver cup, tempering the thin
pulses escaping her lungs.

Her arched eyebrow raises
a too piercing pitch that plummets
to resonance. Now, I inhale with her,
with the woman beside me.
A whole congregation of bodies
takes in the same sanctuary of air.
She stretches a line through us,
the shape of Bach's score translated
into the language of pulse and release.
We share her sheer belief: breathing
is but one act a body might find sacred,
another being stillness, another being song.

Old Women in Eliot Poems

1.
With fine hair on their arms,
with Michelangelo on their lips,
who do not understand the play at all,

not at all, yet still sing such lovely trills,
for someone, and dance rhumbas
on the beach, and pinch sugar cookies

between pale fingers. Go on.
The moonlight and ragtime
will not last. Go on now.

The evening crumbles
like thin dough or sand,
which both taste the same.

2.
Are not so old, too old
but still rather distant.
high up, perhaps in peach

trees that he does not dare
climb, because he stares
down instead at cigarette

butts and lamplight dropped
on streets or bridges, fuller
than he notices. The wild

and wicked rhyme seduces
even the coolest cats
with the deepest blues.

The wicked, deep, wild blues
of the music hall will win.
Look up and sing, for Christ's

sake, look up and moan
in time until a hollow
chapel echoes the sweetest

dying syncopated prayers:
hurry up and live, darling,
hurry up, now, and live.

3

✤

A Map of the Kingdom

"You are not far from the kingdom of God." —Mark 12:34

How near to the borders can we venture,
how close to the looming or invisible walls
    without being taken, trapped like wild game,
    netted like unsuspecting fish that hover
      in their own blue kingdom
    to be suddenly tangled then yanked high
      into a world of light and air?

Some creatures love to be sought, not found,
    love to be caught, not bound,
    to be lured within range,
    never quite aware of where the net
    has cast itself—much wider than we suspect.

Perhaps our sore lips already know the foreign parts of speech.
    Listen. It almost sounds like plainchant.
    Or jazz. An anthem, a cadence
    to coax and measure our steps.

    We should watch where we walk.
    We should watch what we say.

    A kingdom of margins will find us.
    God's grammar is not far from our tongues.

After the Signing of this Sunday's Scripture

"As the Father has loved me, so have I loved you. Now abide in my love."
—John 15:9

The words he forms with his fingers are foreign, to me at least. But they are still Scripture, holy as any words can be. Little intricate gestures and curls of forefinger and thumb, or broad symbols it takes his whole face and shoulder to make, before his hands come to rest at his chest. Somewhere in the flailing, purposeful signs is God.

We sing abide with me, inviting the great gardener, the vintner who prunes back our branching brothers, sisters, selves. Which is the figure? Which the shadow flickering and fired on cave walls? The vineyard, gardener, and sharp lover's blade? Or the long, unfamiliar desire to remain at eventide, to need presence every hour, every single hour?

Ills weigh, not like grapes that hang full in flavor and wait to gush, but heavy, tears with their own bitterness, not like anything, not as anything, not vinegar or bile—just bitter, their own full and hateful flavor.

Remain, abide, prune, grow. They all figure, the figures of speech, today the fingers of speech, the signs, arcing arms and nimble digits, shaped by the helpless, helpless hands that ride the air in ebb and flow, ebb and flow.

He looks to be reaching for what might fill his hands, what figures he might magically grasp, but out here both symbol and silence drip through our cupped palms, through our tight fingers like rain through veined garden leaves, dropping round and hushed into summer dust.

Maundy Thursday, On the Run

"You also ought to wash one another's feet." —John 13:14

To find a body willing is hard. In the mall, I asked old women, young men, a few clerks—could I please wash your feet? I held out a brand new bar of soap and a full blue plastic basin. The pink towel on my shoulder was clean.

And as you might expect, some folks dismissed this as a ploy. A wide man wearing green suggested I kiss his wide ass instead. His leather work boots squeaked against the tile as we each declined the other's gesture.

It was a revelation just how many claimed their feet were plenty clean—tiny women in gossamer shoes; boys in sleek white Nikes; a cop's polished black oxfords shone.

By the time I found someone, the water had grown cold. Yet he only winced a bit at the initial dip of his heel. Callused skin on the balls of his feet and a sharp nail on his big toe kept him from being a stranger. After dabbing dry his skin, I handed him his socks. He knotted up his laces. He asked was it my turn now? But by then I had to run.

Chicken Scratches on the Back of Sunday's Bulletin

"How often I have longed to gather your children together, as a hen gathers her chicks under her wings, but you were not willing."
—Luke 13:34

Off your nest and scrabbling after your offspring,
    who squabble and scramble toward and away
    from you at the slightest signs of foxes or hawks,
    danger or freedom.

Your wings are no eagle's, no dove's, but a simple farm bird's,
    the shedding feathers of a bantam or guinea hen,

Creature raised to be devoured, to lay eggs never intended
    to crack open with life, unless you hide them
    behind a fence post or in a rusted wheelbarrow,
    or pick hard and mean at the hands reaching
    beneath you each afternoon.

Not the strutting, crowing rooster, but the scratching, laying,
    shitting mother of a happenstance, misbred brood.

You clatter noises, warnings, lovings we do not understand
    as we wander and chatter nonsense ourselves
    before returning in fear.

An eagle might kill us; a dove we'd not notice at all.
    Clutch us under your mottled wings.

The Prodigal Mother Suspects

No one, not even Jesus, will mention her,
will imagine her hapless voice, how it sounds
like Sarah, Elizabeth, Martha. She suspected

her husband would give away too much then wait
in the yard like an injured ram. She hears him bleat,
sees him run into the road at every puff of dust.

When he scurries to greet the boy, puts new sandals
on his filthy feet, she knows the party will disturb
her other son, but why not kill livestock? He has plenty.

How content that farmer looks: embracing, chiding,
showing everyone how wide worried arms can open.
No matter who threw away what to begin with,

when a coin, a pearl, a sheep, a son disappears,
she sweeps. She trims a few lamps. She waits
for the end of this parable (or another) to arrive.

Simeon's Ascent

Dust in sunlight slipped into the court with you, child.
    Call and promise ringing on rough stones.

Watchmen wait. Children wait. Prophets cry.
    Old priests, maidens, matrons listen.

    This old heart is not proud or wild.
    eyes glimpse and trace the dark alone,
    except for seeing dust and stone,
    and blessed you, slight suckling child.

    Almost stilled, quiet, as David's
    panting doe, my old, unweaned soul
    has seen salvation. O, Shaddai,
    sweep clean, rebuild this tired court.

    Your servant's suckling, quieted.
    An unweaned watchman, I waited
    for the morning dust in sunlight,
    your whirlwind settled on a child.

Oh God's unsure children, like a weaned child with its mother,
    see the dawning dust of glory and the Gentiles.

Oh children, listen to the call of promise,
    singing in these courtyard stones.

Lydia's Song

"A certain woman named Lydia, a worshipper of God, was listening to us; she was from the city of Thyatira and a dealer in purple cloth."
—Acts 16:14

A heart opens,

    unfolds like a bolt of fine purple cloth.

And there is God,

    wrapped in the body's best linen,
    tangled tight within a woman's woven heart,
    stretched wide to meet the threadbare world.

Veni, Sancte Spiritus

When the broken hearted spirit arrives, no one knows
    how it enters the room,
      what to call the groaning ghost.

It could be flame, could be wind, could be song, or syllables
    arcing on lips like sparks, arching tongues
      to unfamiliar diction, speech so inarticulate and pure.

Wind, flame, words rush over us,
    out of us, in a humiliating gush,
      until the air bears the sounds of wings.

A dove hovers, trapped in our room,
    its rounded, translucent blue head
      dazed against the windows.

God is a small, brown-grey, beautiful bird
    beating wings against unbreachable glass?

The comforter's voice vibrates in the spirit-drunk.
    Shut up and listen. Lift up the sash.

Let the dove loose, a flame to singe the streets and sky.

Let untamed language fall on unsuspecting tongues.

4

♣

A Liturgy for Stones

He answered, "I tell you, if these were silent, the very stones would cry out." —Luke 19:40

1.
Our voices ride the blue flight of morning.

Attend the air until you hear a warning
whistle past your temples and deliver

all God's stained-glass saints. The kneeling,
silent fathers, mothers broken into rivers,

floods of holy slivers, drunken dancers,
baptized by anger. They shudder and sing

on the ridge of liturgy: here is the chance
of a bright morning's rising up to ring

in an old, divine dialect—hard, resonant, unknown—
sharp Pentecost to free the long-staid tongues of stones.

2.
Mercy would be a beginning, so mercy it is, the first word
    to rumble out of the ground,
    to run up, bitter or pure, from a struck open rock.

Hover down, mercy, like a shadow, a long-legged
    shadow to secret bodies from the sun.

An outcropped rock curls like a hand,
    a hollow to hide in, a hollow to die in.

Mercy begins in a desert, runs under bedrock.

Mercy takes a deep drill to vibrate loose.

Mercy juts up sharp and unexpected,
    cuts a trench to catch a downpour,
    low as a gash in the landscape can be
    before becoming a canyon, a gorge, a riverbed.

Justice punctures too deep, rises too high,
    ruins the way for mercy.

So begin. Crack open the earth's crust like bread,
    and ask again for a hard mercy to rise
    between soft hands.

3.
As long as it is day, spread earth over your eyes.
As soon as it is night, burn the mud, dark and hard.

When morning comes, break and crumble the clay.
Let the sky spit light into the dust

until the mask cracks open,
until your salved eyes see.

4.
Whirlwind of drunken dust
    rise and settle,
    rise and fall
        on the cornfields and rice paddies
        on the dirt path and the highway.

Drunken earth, animate with fury, funneled from ground to air
    rise and flee
        to the blood and blue horizon
        to where ground and cloud press against each other
        themselves dancers, legs against legs, torso to torso.

The mountains become sifted sand.

A field is lifted and laid down again.

A body, too, comes from the loam, from the compost
    risen and animated by a whirlwind, by a breath.

A body, again, becomes the compost and dust,
    settled and tamed, settled into bits of bone and soft ash.

5.
How high could a mountain rise? How sharp and hard as a
   mountain peak does a human body wish to be?

The cracks in a face become footholds, handholds, skin clefts
   where three fingertips bear a lover's entire body as she
   leverages her weight to safety. She must swing
   untethered for a time.

What an odd glory bodies might notice if, on random afternoons,
   on a given morning, they attended to a deep crevice,
      pressed their warm
   skin between cool, shaded sandstone or limestone
      and peered down, and
   heard the coursing, unbidden stream report and
      resolve in a mountain's hidden gaps.

And on earth,   and under the earth
rivulets cut paths to the center,   dissect dust into canyons.
And above the unfertile clay   good-will falls in torrents,
eroding topsoil,   filling the basins,
flooding riverbeds,   smoothing jagged rock.

And this is praise, an echo,   an invective, a blessing,
a worn thanksgiving of water,   duet of water and rock,
sprays of whitewater,   pools without undertow,
harrowing blessing beneath,   and beneath all blessing

               a stone.

6.
Beyond all blessing and hoping, beyond worry
    and all the wonders ever spoken in the world,

Behind all the masquerading temples and pillars,
    an echo, an impassive prayer.

Hear the one voice, the separate voice
    reverberate from alabaster and from gold,
    return from granite and from greenstone,
    ascend from the deltas and the faults,
    rest in the floodplain and the desert.

This voice, established and rugged, thinner
    than you have imagined.

This voice, incomprehensible and firm, sharper,
    than you have imagined.

The cathedral and the tiny cell cannot contain
    this resonant love.

It adorns the rubble, addresses the scattered, assembles the lost.

You must be hammered brass to vibrate.

You must be a hollow cylinder of hardened clay.

You must be a sculpted masterpiece pressed to powder by time.

You must become rubble to absorb this resonant love.

7.
One maker of atmosphere and ground.

A lover of concrete, crushed and gathered.

Two weary hands that scour and abrade the fields,

wide and slow as the glaciers that carry an erratic gift
    to the world's most fertile prairie.

A molten blaze of light to show the blood stained rocks
    along Babylon's shore, along Nicaraguan rivers,
    on Dutch bricks, already red,
    or bones appearing and vanishing in Saharan sands.
    Outside Beijing, trees fire down roots into the oldest walls.

And we look for a resurrection,
and we hope for a resurrection,
of the solid world to come.

8.
Our voices arrive in a carnival, cacophony of pleasure
that dissolves into a monotone, then empty air.

We've built no sturdy home, no well-laid road. They require
hands and a history of steady hands for hire.

But remember the first blue morning when you heard
the deep cadence of the earth? The poem you blurt

Into the evening will not last. The guitar and drum
and the entire choir that seem so solid will all come

down to more than you can rest on your tongue.
Sing and sing. And when you cannot raise a note of song,

the rocks will cry out. And when the echoing stones go still,
in the dangerous crevice that is your heart, if you lie still,

there remains an altar, a way to enter
a terrible holiness, a lush and delicate calm.

5

♣

Suburban Art

We need poems like lattes,
frothy, hot, and four
dollars each. No more
bone hard poems to break
more bones on. No bitter,
cheap drive-thru coffee
poems. We need them
smooth as steamed milk
and Italian espresso
ready to sip through
a plastic lid. We love
a cardboard sleeve
to protect our hands
from the cardboard heat.

No more small children
dying. No teeth missing
unless a fairy
can place dollars
under the pillow,
bills folded like love.

No more poems that smell
like urine in subways,
that shiver, or punch
a fist to the jaw.
No. We want a strip
mall full of pretty
poems—to go with sofas
and to play on large
screens, on stereos.

We want lovers who meet,
clandestine, at coffee
shops and do not tell
on each other. No more
pissed off, rhyming, hip
hop, fleshy, world weary
poems. No. We need poems
like handshakes. We want
a smooth poem, a paved
home, and two turn lanes.
We want to park between
the yellow lines.

Let all the suburban
souls wear soft leather
gloves and hum poems
together, sip in unison,
delicately without making
too damned much noise.

When I Stay Home from Church

I kneel to lift the Tribune, rolled thick as a human leg,
    unfold it, the world creased and nestled inside itself,
    unscattered, unread in my lap.

A white mug warms my hands,
    like a just-woken lover's skin.

Around the neighborhood, I process
    past the blonde brick L of the ranch next door,
    pick up a gallon of milk at the White Hen.

I celebrate a bowl of Cheerios, attend to the television,
    homiletics of shrewd doves and innocent hawks.

My body wilts and drips clean after an hour's bath.

Oh, anoint my head with strawberry shampoo.

I towel my bare self dry, a limb at a time.

And as I trim my wild beard in the steamed mirror,
    the razor hums a pedal tone, so I pretend
    I can render a Bach chorale, "O Sacred Head,"
    all four parts, alone.

Sunday Afternoon in the Universe

Your Grandmother's bones are turning to dust.
After ninety years, she cannot trust
them as they strand her in a bed
she will one day leave, with rickety

or resurrected bones. My God, she lies,
restless, miles away, while we make love
with shades drawn, television loud enough
to keep our small child from hearing wonders

and tragedies, to keep her from waking too soon.
She rests. She grows her body's own way.
I want to tell someone who needs to hear
how our bodies, these flawed, fair bodies

might come together on Sunday afternoons,
even while another's flesh and muscle fail.
How strong and fragile human bones and skin
and breath make us, leave us. I would tell you,

but you know better than to believe me. I should make
the words for another woman, a man, a girl, a boy.
Perhaps they have forgotten or not yet found their form
is not theirs. It belongs to universes of cells, of blood,

of oxygen, of stars, of dust, of molecules like galaxies,
of galaxies like molecules that swirl and mingle to save
and kill, love and forget, find and lose us, suddenly,
in our own or others' bodies, on Sunday afternoons.

The Former Tenant Leaves No Forwarding Address

How urgent her stacks of mail appear:
possible checks, certain bills, a sizable batch
of trust fund material in mint green envelopes,
and, today, her summons for jury duty.
You should go, I tell my wife. Show up,
swear you're her, take along her copy of *Glamour*
and read those five tips to drive me wild in bed;
her new man will miss out, but we can pretend.
When they call her name, declare everyone
innocent. I'll be here, opening the rest of our mail.

A Line

It is early, before work,
and a woman's pressed skirt
ripples as if it were water.
So the man making breakfast
imagines swimming in a line,
arms alternately angled,
head cocking right, eyes open.
If he is careless, he will burn
the toast or pour too much
cream in her coffee as he knifes
through his mind's empty pool.
Ah, he says, aloud. The stitch
ripped through the water heals
too quickly as she turns,
taking the cup and plate he offers.
Her hips and the fabric catch
in each other's wake. He rolls
his neck hard to the left.
His mouth opens, a reflex.
If he could breathe

Swimming Lesson

When she pinches her nose shut and has plunged
her face into the water, I hold my breath.

My hands and arms tense, legs set to lunge
forward and down into the filmy brown

Youghiogheny circling my calves. In seconds
she lifts from the river and shakes out

wet, brown curls ironed straight by the water.
She would have done just as well without me.

She tilts her head back until her hair trails
in the current. She flips the whip ends to one side

and for an instant a woman stands full before me
where a four year old should be. Some boy,

some damned boy will try some warm or cold day
to see what I know now. Beauty swells and rides

streams beyond control. I want to whisper
into her innermost ear what she will never hear:

Make that boy hold his breath until he hurts,
until the cold water cripples his knees and hands.

If he loves you like this, he just may
sink or dive into your wake, gasping,

and following you right into rapids.
Even if he loves you like this, swim away.

A Selfish Sonnet of Thanksgiving

A cluttered, quiet home, paper stacked high
on every horizontal plane or chair.
A child whose greatest trial is her hair,
tangled without mercy, every day. Why
not sing slight psalms of gratitude when light
pours onto hardwood floors? Or when coffee
scents the middle of the day? I can see
from this window twenty sturdy, square white
homes where grief arrives at night on colored
screens that one deft finger can transform to
happiness with a click. I say thank you
these jeans pockets hold just four creased dollars,
and when my wife comes through the kitchen door
we argue about laundry and not war.

The Poet Keeps an Easter Vigil

What a lousy night to write about war,
to be faithful and trace hope like a scar
that every reader will notice, at worst
will consider a trick of the work, burst
of pale light to save a poem that would
be better off wounded. Tonight how could
our vigil end otherwise? How I'd rather
wince at the world exploding or gather
reason around God like a batch of tanks.
we could pop pop pop a few rounds. No thanks,
for the scant resurrection. And when spring
arrives in Jerusalem, no doves sing.
So write nothing but cupped hands, leaving room,
a poem held open, a dark gaping tomb.

Silence, 11 September 2001

To mark the many names of terror
To imagine (always away) a flaming wing
To hear the uttered absences of prayer
To bear the surgeon's sharpest sting
To love the gun-metal taste of vengeance
To bite back the bitter tongue of revenge
To wash away the ashes of God from our eyes.

Afterword

✤

Poems Should Not Be

About protest marches,
about newspaper photographs,

(even if the man shielding his son from bullets has a name,
and looks eternal, even if the blood dipped hands, spread wide
at the window, look eternal)

about elections, about television screens,
about fathers, especially, dead ones,

about domestic tasks, about vices,
about children, about God, about paintings,

(enough with mystery and art, divinity tucked into words,
mucked onto canvas, enough with epiphanies in museums
or churches, on roads and old barstools)

about drinking hard, about getting hard,
about getting lucky, about waking up unexpectedly calm,

(already seen that man's round, unwieldy stomach, this woman's
delicate breast, already known the sweat and wine scent of
bodies in the morning)

about worry, about worry, about worry,
about flowers, about, especially, roses,

about what will be missed by the living,
about what will be missed by the dead,

(too many anecdotes, devoid of music, devoid of rhythm,
devoid, too many parables, disguised as music, disguised as
rhythm, disguised)

about poetry, about language,
about reading, about poetry.

Poems should not be about.

Notes

Altar Piece is in memory of Sven Josefson.

Children's Sermon is for First Mennonite Church, Urbana, Illinois.

At the Mennonite Talent Show is for Perry Biddle.

Looking at Roadside Bluestem Before Leaving Decatur is for former students and colleagues at Richland Community College.

Gammal Fäbodpsalms refers to an old pastoral hymn made internationally famous by the Swedish composer Oskar Lindberg. Fabodpsalms were traditionally sung by women as they tended cattle and sheep. *Småland* is a central agricultural region of Sweden. *Illinois sea* was a popular image in the writings of early European settlers to the Midwest. See, for instance, Eliza Farnham's *Life in Prairie Land.*

Blind Willie's Wife draws on the life of the early blues and gospel singer Blind Willie Johnson who helped pioneer slide guitar and whose wife often accompanied him on recordings. *Broke bottlenecks for him* is a mention of the early guitarist's practice of using the necks of bottles as slides. The *glass dust* on Willie's shoes belongs to Eric Woodgates. This poem is for Ron Jones.

After Bach's Air in G is for flutist Jill Burlingame.

After the Signing of This Sunday's Scriptures is for Bruce Miller and Janet Fros.

A Liturgy for Stones blends (and bends) several liturgical models including the traditional mass (especially *Bach's Mass in b minor*), The Liturgy of the Hours, and the Jewish prayer of Kaddish. Section 2 adapts the Kyrie from the mass, Section 5 the Gloria, and Section 7 the Credo. Section 6 borrows liberally from the Kaddish.

Suburban Art owes its genesis to Amiri Baraka's "Black Art."

Swimming Lesson is set in the *Youghiogheny*, a river in southwestern Pennsylvania.